FEELING BLUE

FEELING BLUE

by Robert Jay Wolff

Charles Scribner's Sons
New York

To Wendy, Pedro, and Guy

BLUE

IS A SHY COLOR

COMPARED TO RED

YELLOW, BLUE,
AND RED
ARE PRIMARY
COLORS

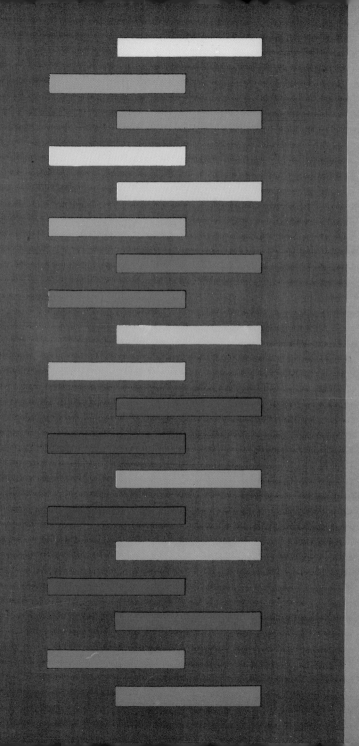

ALL OTHER
COLORS
ARE MADE
WITH THEM

BLUE IS A COLOR OF MANY NAMES AND MOODS

INDIGO   VIOLET   LAVENDER

CERULEAN   COBALT   ULTRAMARINE

BLUE CAN BE COLD AS AN ARCTIC ICEBERG

WARM AS A TROPICAL SEA

BLUE CAN DO

MANY THINGS OTHER COLORS CANNOT DO

FOR INSTANCE

BLUE **CAN MAKE** RED **SEE**

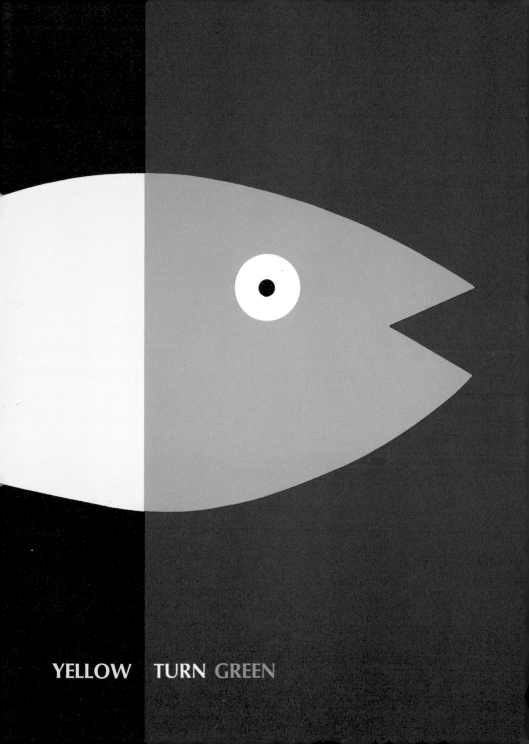

YELLOW TURN GREEN

DARK BLUE AND GREEN
ARE FRIENDLY COLORS

YET BRIGHT BLUE AND RED
ALWAYS FIGHT EACH OTHER

IN THE CIRCLE OF COLORS,
BLUE AND ORANGE ARE OPPOSITES,
BUT THEY LOOK WELL TOGETHER

MIX BLUE AND ORANGE
AND THEY TURN BROWN

STUFFY LADIES
ARE SOMETIMES CALLED

"BLUESTOCKINGS"

GRUMPY GENTLEMEN
ARE SOMETIMES CALLED "BLUENOSES"

WHEN THINGS GO WRONG, PEOPLE OFTEN SAY
THEY ARE "FEELING BLUE"

BLUE CAN BE A CHEERFUL COLOR, TOO

ONE LOOK AT THE BLUE SKY ON A SUMMER DAY
AND YOU CAN'T HELP

FEELING GAY